SUNSPOTS

Simon Barraclough is originally from Yorkshire and has lived in London since 1997. His debut collection, *Los Alamos Mon Amour*, was a Forward Prize finalist in 2008. In 2010 he published a pamphlet of commissioned poems, *Bonjour Tetris* (Penned in the Margins), and his second full collection, *Neptune Blue* (Salt Publishing), followed in 2011. He has contributed regularly to BBC Radio's The Verb and The Film Programme, as well as to The Long View. In 2014, Simon was writer in residence at UCL's Mullard Space Science Laboratory in Surrey. He is very excited about our neighbourhood star.

ALSO BY SIMON BARRACLOUGH

POETRY

Los Alamos Mon Amour (Salt Publishing, 2008)
Bonjour Tetris (Penned in the Margins, 2010)
Neptune Blue (Salt Publishing, 2011)
The Debris Field with Chris McCabe and Isobel Dixon (Sidekick Books, 2013)

AS EDITOR

Psycho Poetica (Sidekick Books, 2012)
Laboratorio (Sidekick Books, 2015)

Sunspots

Simon Barraclough

Penned in the Margins

LONDON

PUBLISHED BY PENNED IN THE MARGINS
Toynbee Studios, 28 Commercial Street, London E1 6AB
www.pennedinthemargins.co.uk

First published 2015

Printed in the United Kingdom by Berforts Information Press Ltd.

ISBN
978-1-908058-26-3

Supported using public funding by
ARTS COUNCIL
ENGLAND
LOTTERY FUNDED

Sunspots

Sunspots are generated and decay in longer and shorter periods; some condense and others greatly expand from day to day; they change their shapes, and some of these are most irregular; there their obscurity is greater and there less.

Galileo Galilei, letter to Mark Welser, 4th May 1612

I am ashamed
To look upon the holy sun, to have
The benefit of his blest beams, remaining
So long a poor unknown.

William Shakespeare, *Cymbeline*

The Sun woke me this morning
with a swift kick to the door,
its rays full with a breakfast tray
rattling with silverware,
orange juice and sunny-sides-up,
and crisped toast slathered
with butter fattened on all that grass,
saying, "Hey! Budge up,
let me slide in alongside,
it's a whiteout outside,
the schools are closed,
the roads are glazed in bottle-ice,
no-one's going anywhere today."

⊙

My mistress' eyes are nothing like the Sun;
they *are* the Sun, and make a sundial of my gait.
Too late each pace and all my mornings gone,
I'm hanging on, rattling the abacus, totting up
the setting Suns I have to come.

⊙

Could it have known —
as the disc accrued,
as gravity drew all things to itself,
as proto-planets formed
in its skirts,
came spinning like googlies
from the back of the maker's hand —
that it would have to oversee all this,
the billion years of agony
and bliss
the Sun-kissed flyblown wounds of everything that exists?

⊙

Photon, get a move on.
A million years or more
pushing through the crowds,
from the core;
not sure I can wait eight minutes more
for you to speed through space
and hit my eye.
Penetrate me, little one,
see right through me,
screen your favourite movies
in my skull,
light my way from east to west.
My usherette.

⊙

For I will consider my Star Sol.

For I am the servant of this Living God and daily serve her.

For at the first glance of the glory of God in the East I worship in
my way.

For this is done by fixing espresso and watching the pinkening light
on The Shard.

For then she waves her warmth across the scene and lifts the hearts
of those who took a Night Bus at 4 a.m. to clean HQs.

For she tickles the orbitals of foxes in their stride and hies them
home.

For having risen and settled into her groove she begins to consider
herself.

For this she performs in eleven degrees.

For first she does the Planck to strengthen core stability.

For secondly she runs a malware scan for comets closing in.

For thirdly she completes the paperwork for eclipses total, annular
and partial.

For fourthly: flares.

For fifthly she sorts her sunspots into pairs.

For sixthly she gives neutrinos Priority Boarding.

For seventhly she referees the arm-wrestling match between the
upstart fusion and gravity.

For eighthly she weaves flux ropes and thinks up skipping games.
For ninthly she degausses her plasma screens.
For tenthly she is profligate with her photons.
For eleventhly: star jumps.
For having considered herself she will consider her neighbours.
For she runs a cloth around the ecliptic to make it gleam.
For she oils the wheels of any planets gliding there.
For she sends invites out to wallflowers in the Oort cloud.
For she issues shadows for children to dodge as they make their
        way to school.
For she shakes out her blankets for devotees of helioseismology.
For when she takes her prey she plays with it to give it a chance.
For one planet in nine escapes by her dallying.
For in her morning orisons she loves the Earth and the Earth loves
        her.
For she is of the tribe of Tyger! Tyger!
For she hands out colouring books to chameleons in the morning.
For when it is time to rise she blushes to be seen at so intimate an
        hour.
For when it is time to set she is crimson ashamed to run out on us.
For though she neither rises nor sets she thinks it best that we believe
so, so that we can take our rest and fuel our waking with
        anticipation.

For she lifts oceans over mountains without thinking.

For she tries to solve the puzzle of the weather, placing *this* here
and *that* there and attempts to even out the air.

For she is a mixture of gravity and waggery.

For she's a stickler for solstices.

For she booms like a woofer for those that can hear.

For she cares not what lives as long as all live.

For she takes her time.

For she lenses the light from distant stars to swerve it into our
sockets.

For sometimes in the winter haze she's as pale as a lemon drop and
lets us watch her bathe unpunished.

For she never calls in sick.

For her colours are open-source.

For every raindrop's an excuse for Mardi Gras,

For she will work on her drafts for a million years and release them
typo-free.

For she will lash out and then regret the hurt.

For she promises radio hams jam tomorrow.

For your power grid is a cobweb she walks into when she steps off
her porch.

For she kept mum through the Maunder Minimum.

For her behaviour is definitely 'on the spectrum'.

For she keeps dark about dark matter but she definitely knows
   something.
For she plays Miss Prism in *The Importance of Being Furnaced*.
For she offers board and lodging to Turner's 'Angel in the Sun'.
For she made a great figure in Egypt for her signal services.
For she can fuse the wounded parts of a broken heart and release
   the lost mass as hope.
For she spins plates to create auroras.
For she leaves clues all over the place: some cryptic, some quick,
   some general knowledge-based.
For she is hands-off.
For she tends to micro-manage.
For she lays down squares of light for your pets to sleep in.
For she turns a blind eye to all the creeping, swooping killers of the
   night but leaves a Moon-faced night-light on.
For her sunquakes flatten no buildings, gridlock no cities, disgorge
   no refugees.
For she is not too proud to dry your smalls.
For she gives us heliopause and time to rethink disastrous
   decisions.
For Ray-Bans.

For she polarises opinion.

For her secrets are waiting to free us.

For she appreciates Stonehenge and visits every day.

For she sets herself by the grid of Manhattan.

For she will kill you with the loving of you.

For she can shine.

⊙

Mercury's right up in my face,
Venus is a hellish place,
Earth has caught the human race,
Mars is just a basket case,
Jupiter's girth is a disgrace,
Saturn twirls with dancer's grace,
Uranus is rather base,
Neptune plods at wretched pace,
Pluto is now lost in space.

⊙

Hail Etna, full of fire, the heat is with thee; blessed art thou amongst mountains, and blessed is the fruit of thy maw, Lava. Holy Etna, Handmaiden of Sol, spray for us sinners, now and at the hour of our setting.

⊙

The brick-kilned air walls me in.
Who on earth could work in this?
Across town aircon units fail
and editors bin my emails in the glare
of UV and VDU.

Neighbours char on lounger
and deckchair, railway tracks sigh
and liquefy and someone leaves
their baby without a crack of air
in a baking Ford Fiesta.

Figurines slip from their plinths
in Madame Tussauds. Gaga
plants her waxen rump
into Winston Churchill's softening hands
and they slump to the floor.

⊙

It pleases me to quicken the critters,
to heat the scales and singe the feathers,
to tickle the old skin-deep precursors
and rev up the Vitamin D.

Through the canopy of leaves I see
a serpent so hot-headed
he's spitting fire with forkèd tongue
and he's eager to talk to anyone.

⊙

Unsundownable.

Like Jupiter on speed.

The season's hottest ticket.

If you only orbit one main sequence star this year, make it this one.

Like Jupiter on crack.

I started watching at sunrise and was still watching by sunset.

Will linger with you long after the last ray.

It's Proxima Centauri meets Beta Pictoris.

Confirms the Sun as our system's most creative star.

Like Jupiter on crystal meth.

Our greatest living hydrogen stylist.

Once you've tasted helium, you won't want to go back to hydrogen.

A luminous debut.

At its core lies a fusion of hydrogen, hydrogen, hydrogen and
       hydrogen.

Will appeal to the dedicated Sun lover and casual astronomer alike.

At a push, I'd have to say
that Vincent was my fave,
despite his weakness for starry nights,
those mirrors of wheat,
the gnawing gristle of existential...
well, you know what I mean:
that soggy stuff in the middle of you people.

Remember my tussle with the wind
to get the traveller to remove his coat
and the wind smote and stupidly smote
and I wooed with waves of woozy heat?

Well, it was just the same with Vince.
Remove the vestiges, hack through sinew,
scimitar the ear: a cinch.
Then send the iron through the heart
inch by superheated inch.

⊙

Komorebi streams
the untranslatable light
through leaves of language.

⊙

I take my responsibility
for these rocky, gassy charges
seriously, as you can see,
but sometimes I yearn to cut my ties
and leave to join the Pleiades,
the bright blue-hot sorority that flees
Orion's bow.
                    If it were up to me, I'd go,
but
the
gravitarchy.

The Flat Earth Society
eventually
dropped its core belief
to much relief
but still insists the Sun is flat
and shineysheer as gold leaf,
orbiting our newly plumped-up sphere.

⊙

The universe hurts.
But you knew that.

I pity you your brief lives:
over in the squint of an eye.
It's a problem
but don't overblink it.

Some stars are shy:
the distant ones,
the clingy, binary ones,
the dense ones who try to swallow
their own tails of light
but lack the mass,
didn't get the right start in life.

Step forward,
feel the warmth.

I'll let you in on a secret.
Hell is just an oven pre-heating
for something *really* wicked
coming this way.

Turn around for your shadow.
What do you see?
Four legs, two legs, three?
How limpingly Oedipal you can be.

Ever want to be a star?
It's a simple recipe —
most households have the ingredients.
Everyone has a shelfful of dead cells,
an old bag of gravity
trapped at the back of the pantry.
You just don't have enough
of what it takes.

Is Jupiter a failed star
or an over-achieving planet?
You decide.
Put *your* spin on it.

Stars are the Yes Men of the universe.
No negative capability.
Four billion years of saying "Yes"
and five billion years of "Yeses" yet to come.

I'd love to use up this core,
begin to mumble "Maybe" for a trillion years or more.

I pity you your brief lives.
Are you planning for your nebula?
The things you'll leave behind.
Your inventory,
memento mori.

The universe hurts.
But you knew that.
(I'm starting to repeat myself,
my daddy was a pulsar.)
Poor steadfast Keats knew it.

I spent a million years
making one perfect photon
to send to the Spanish Steps
the dawn they carried him down.

A star will never let you down
but a planet will break your heart.

⊙

The Atacama Cell collected chemicals,
sent encrypted emails
and buried used SIM cards
in sour Camorra landfills.

With their sights on seven billion
they cooked up a sunblock,
factor one million,
careful to leave at night,
suicide solarnauts,
aiming to rub out the Sun.

They stowed away on the final shuttle
where we found them huddled
with tubes and bottles,
in tin foil jump suits and shades.
Now they live in darkness in orange onesies.

⊙

At a push, I'd have to say
that Joseph was my fave,
although he held me at paintbrush's length all his long days
and swaddled me in oily clouts
or set me hanging in the rigging
of some shattered ship of sky
to be doused by hurricanoes, water spouts;
you know the kind of thing.

But in the end,
like many on the brink of sleep,
he conjured me until I seemed to sear his eyes
and that's where I, finally,
reside.

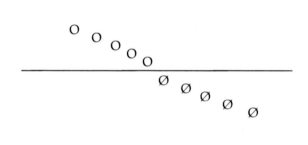

Troms

⊙

Ø	is a newborn crowning
Ø	is its first non-word
Ø	is a hand over the mouth
Ø	is a stud through the tongue
Ø	is a cloud over the Moon
Ø	is a blade across the eye
Ø	is a shower curtain yanked
Ø	is your first little lie
Ø	is a cautionary tale
Ø	is a vow you will break
Ø	is a stalled Ferris wheel
Ø	is Cupid's target
Ø	is a fertilised egg
Ø	is a new mutation
Ø	is the Sun having set
Ø	is the first song of death

⊙

These dark spots: cooler slots
for the fingers of Orion
should he choose to bowl
these ninepins,
the whole danged solar bang shoot,
into the pit.

⊙

Forget your fusion and your photons,
your particle≈wave shenanigans.
We plucked a sun and peeled its rind
and found inside it's powered not by furnaces
but recollected Christmases.

⊙

Mercury has got no friends,
Venus climbs and then descends,
Earth was ruled by Father Thames,
Mars will never make amends,
Jupiter's gravity defends,
Saturn's ringed by odds and ends,
Uranus tries not to offend,
Neptune's a lost blue contact lens,
Pluto's tenure's at an end.

At a push, I'd have to say
that Miró was my fave.
His gaze never left
that inner sunset;
his watch never let me off
the hook; that look towards
the thing I've heard you talk
about, the thing that waits,
that red, red, red, red, thing,
that fate. I watched him paint
The Happiness of Loving My Brunette
and felt a twinge of regret.
I watched his tapestry trashed
among three thousand souls.
He made art worth destroying,
I guess.

I had a dream, which was not all a dream.
The Moon and stars were extinguish'd and the Sun
Was stalled at its zenith and ceased to move,
Blazing and burning, and the flinching Earth
Shrank parched and black'ning in the Moonless air.
Dusk came and went — and came, and brought no night,
And men forgot their passions in the light
Of this their desolation; and all their hearts
Were broiled into a selfish prayer for dark;
And they did live under blackout curtains
And the thrones, the palaces of crowned kings,
The habitations of all things which dwell
Were stripped of wood and cloth for barriers;
Cities withered and were consumed by fire
As precious water turned to steam and rushed
Into the air that shimmered with a killing glare,
And men and women and children dare not
Step out into the light that singed their hair,
And lasered through the papery lids
That barely covered o'er their eyes which shrunk
Into their sockets, blank and seared, as if
Some wicked child took them for insects
And scorched cruel spots onto their flesh

With a magnifying glass, for sport;
And vehicles exploded randomly
To increase the general heat and harm,
And thirsting wretches dug into the earth
With splintering nails and breaking fingers,
Groping for a seam of sodden soil on which
To suck, or fistful of worms that might give up
Some still-trapped moisture; happy were those
Who worked underground in mines or transport
Systems and knew where stores were kept,
And knew where the best drips dripped and knew where
Best to block the entrances; a fearful hope
Was all the world contain'd: forests burst into flame
And quickly worked to join the towns and cities
In fearful conurbation of conflagration;
And every wooden dwelling was ash and every
Concrete dwelling was so hot that none
Could stay inside and soon the streets were mobbed
By families and lonely wanderers
Ghosting through the streets under makeshift rags.
And all the time the Sun stood proud and smote
Its total power on the ground, hammering
The anvil of the Earth and forging Death

Into one blazing sword of punishment.
The brows of men in the merciless light
Were simply gone: burned off or rubbed away
By agitated fingers trying to trap and
Neutralise the glare; overheated creatures
Roamed the streets to snatch all scraps of cover,
Leaving naked children on the road to bake
And char in the oven of unstoppable
Rays and, sad to say, more scurried from the dark
Of starving nooks and corners to snatch away
The half-cooked babes whose aromatic flesh
And reservoirs of liquid blood o'ercame
The last remains of civilised restraint;
And all the fields were dust, and all the streams
Were dust, and all the woods were dust, and all
The parks were dust, and all the private pools
Were dust, and all the iron in the veins
Of men and women and children was rust;
And birds dropped from the sky with feathers
Melted to their sides, the wildest brutes came tame
And tremulous and half-blind, and vipers crawl'd
And twin'd themselves among the multitude,
Hissing, but stingless, and all were slain for food.

And War, which for a moment was no more,
Did glut itself again under the light,
The superheated canopy that promised
All would see the filthy Sun-flayed deeds
As if the whole world were a plasma screen
And every messy murder by jihadist
Or pensioned soldier had 10 billion hits
And made some kind of sense, some difference,
But not a whit: only blood and cum and tears
Irrigated these new deserts. And rumours
Started of a dark world, of a hemisphere
Where no Sun shone, where purple flowers bloomed
Under the Moon, and water rained from stars
And books were read again in pallid light
And eyes found rest and limbs relaxed and lips
Remembered how to kiss; and they filled ships
And boats and rafts and paddled, rowed and sailed
To the horizon over sunken seas
That trickled to bed-rock and ocean cave
And ripp'd their keels from under them and still
The Sun refused to move and burned their bones
Clean through their flesh to chalk and calcium;
All Earth was but one thought — and that was death.

The world was void, a famished, loveless coal,
Shadowless, seasonless, treeless, manless,
Womanless, childless, lifeless, hopeless,
A nub of death — a tablet of baked clay.
The rivers, lakes and oceans were no more,
And nothing stirr'd on scalded ocean floor,
Nor predator, nor scudding prey, nor scavenger,
Nor carrion relieved the blankness of dead land;
No breeze could shift, no thermal lift, no light
Relent, no passing cloud provide relief;
The Sun stared down with hateful eye upon
The bleaching scene and never blinked and never
Glanced away and never let night take the place
Of day.

⊙

How's my coal getting on?
I set as much aside as I could for you.
Don't use it all at once.
It should come in handy one day.

How's my oil faring?
It keeps best in the dark, underground.
Doesn't do so well in the light.
Don't let it spoil.

I assume you're using solar, right?
The other stuff's for back-up.
Just in case there's a rainy day
for me, in space.

The thing about God is you can't look at Her.
She solders the optic nerve, blacks out
the tricksy motherboard of sanity.

Where is She?
Let's have a look-see.

Sunny Henry met   the day,
indefatigable Henry shone.
I see his point, — a trying to win things over.
It was the thought that they thought
they could *do* it made Henry happy and away.

All the world like a puppy's chew toy
once did seem in Henry's cot.
Then came a departure.
Thereafter all did tumble forth as it might or would.
I don't see how Henry, pie-eyed
for the world to see, could stay inside.

What he has now to say is a long
wonder: the world stuffed wif beauty.
Once in a gas cloud I was glad
all in the midst, and I sang.
Bright on the land beam the strong rays
and busy grows every sea.

We are as jealous as Swann of the stars,
of what they're doing out there in the dark,
of whom they're seeing behind our backs
when they have sent us home *sans cattleya*
to our lonely flats, where we realise
that all that ice-hot charm we took for ours
is radiating on the spectrograph
of a rival's smile, the neat rows of teeth,
the absorption lines in their irises.
Although it's late, and it humiliates,
we take a black cab back and wait outside
her window, watching shadows flux the light
through the shutters, to and fro, to and fro:
we find the exoplanet that kills us.

⊙

Kintsukuroi
solders golden filaments
cherishes repair.

Let there be Lo-Lee-Light of my loins.
The Sun of my infancy had set
and I dissolved in the Sun, with my book,
Sun-bathing on the so-called 'piazza'
as they tried to blot out the Sun, and she
tossed it up into the Sun-dusted air, and caught it.
The implied Sun pulsated in the supplied poplars,
and the Sun was on her lips, and her lips
were already riding into the low morning Sun.
The gesture proved to be like a distant and terrible Sun
and the red Sun of desire and decision
came out of a Sun-dappled privy marked 'Women.'
I knew the Sun shone because my ignition key
stood there, shining in the Sun and the dog
and the Sun and the shade and the wet
and the weak and the strong and the stone, Sun-coloured
above a picnic table with Sun flecks, in some little town
in the Sun Valley of Idaho before a brick hotel,
in faded slacks, passed by in the Sun and,
slitting my Sun-speared eyes, the pavonine
Sun was all eyes and I had gloated over
the Sun-shot, watered, damp-smelling sidewalks
of ancient Europe. A cold wet Sun had sidled out,

every vehicle under the dancing Sun would
hang in the Sun for a second, myself crying
from a doorway into the Sun, with the acoustics
of time, domed time, in the camouflage of Sun and shade
as if the Sun had gone out of the game. Lo slackened
and her topaz ring burned in the Sun, with
the Sun on her beloved legs. All at once
the Sun was visible again. Let there be.
Let her be light. Let her be. Let her be.

⊙

Your careless boyfriend,
half-uninterested,
has left a shape of skin
upon your shoulder
unprotected,
unsunblocked.

I'll work all day on that tender, precious spot.

⊙

Mercury is fleet of foot,
Venus is knee-deep in soot,
Earth's a painful paper cut,
Mars would love to be a slut,
Jupiter has a massive butt,
Saturn has a satellite glut,
Uranus took one to the nut,
Neptune chugs around, phut phut,
Pluto's one of us, but...

⊙

Did you hear?
The Sun's on lithium —
has been for years.

Every star I ever knew
was wildly bipolar.
Magnetic, but messed up.

Take one errant planet
every few billion years.
If symptoms persist,
see your spectrometrist.

⊙

There's no hiding behind chlorpromazine,
which sucks your bones,
like sticks of rock,
to needle points;
which plants its knee upon your throat,
scrimshaws your jaw
with a frieze from de Sade;
fumbles out your eyes
with a melon baller
and stuffs camphor-laden tufts
of cotton wool in there to stem
the bloody visions;
which cranks your eyelids through
a pasta maker, each sheet thinner,
seethroughier,
then lays them on a noonday rock
to crisp; which flips you on your back
and arches you above an arrowhead,
leaving you to sigh, to slide onto the tip
which pushes daisies through
the garden of your ribs
and smokes in the shimmering air,
a red torch-lily dipped in blood.

At a push, I'd have to say
that Seurat was my fave,
divining the prism
through Divisionism,
apportioning the visible
particle by particle;
a little dotty perhaps,
pointedly finishing
that damned hat.

I liked to spend Sunday
in the park with George,
making my entrance again
with my usual flare.

Dogs and monkeys and parasols.
"Let's go and get drunk
on light again. It consoles."

I wasn't always so solo,
I had a partner once —
let's call her Nemesis.

She said I was selfish,
too heliocentric; she
slept with a comet.

We went from binary
to ornery,
our relationship a
broke orrery.

⊙

Mercury has a massive core,
Venus is a lusty whore,
Earth's the real bringer of war,
Mars is feeling saddle sore,
Jupiter's a crashing bore,
Saturn hates to be ignored,
Uranus is a frozen haw,
Neptune is all ocean floor,
Pluto is a minus score.

⊙

Like many poets these days, I do a lot of prism work: going into prisms, getting a sense of the reality of prism life, finding out what it's like for different wavelengths in prism. Prisms are tough places: all those frequencies jammed in, herded together like there's nothing to distinguish them, like they're all just one homogenised mass of white light. There's a lot of angst among the angstroms. I go into prisms and try to give the individual wavelengths a voice, you know? We role-play, we act out, we workshop, we assemble texts, we improv scripts, we palimpsest, we perform at 'slammers'. And sometimes these acts of self-expression spill out of the prism, onto the streets.

⊙

Red or dead?
I've got no choice.
I'm afeared of the object
in the rear-view mirror:
my future, tailgating.
Within each red apple
wriggles the worm
of vermillion, the vermin-
Hydra hungrily hollowing.
When my time comes
I will blush to display
such loss, I will push
you away, will not let you
commiserate over my red body.

▲

Orange got its gear on
and went to go earn
a crust from the crust, an ogre
fracking lands where its ego ran

amok, unpicking mineral seams to nag ore
from beauty we thought would not wither nor age.

▲

You Judas hue.
Giallo.
Stalker of women,
twister of plots
and knives.

Jealous zealot, splitting
on the prism, ratting
on the rest, wheedling
the whole colour wheel
to hearsay and heresy.

Such duplicity, and yet you yell
Look at me!
Look at me!
Look at me!

▲

Green, ever keen, seethes synergy;
never been peeved, keeps bees,
esteems Greensleeves; seeks even keels,
flees defenceless lest spleen wheels,
exceeds then feels energy seep.

▲

Blue straggler,
don't be sad,
and do try to keep up.

▲

Indigo should go:
never did it,
shouldn't be here,
was a fit-up,
had cast iron alibis,
was picked out
from a line-up
standing between
violet and blue;
what you gonna do?
Let indigo.

▲

Violet violent as an 'ultra'
or inviolate as a saint?

The reverb from a viola
playing purple passages.

A Parma Violet on your tongue,
like the contents of your grandma's handbag,

reminding you that childhood
is neither sweet nor sour

and never tastes quite right;
the elusive *umami* of mommy and daddy.

A triolet seems apposite
but th'imperial cloak

will not be hemmed by this pattern,
will not colour inside the lines.

Better daub the darkness of caves,
mumble morosely in mauve,

crack the shells of sea snails,
extract some unseeable snaily gland

and set its juice in the Sun's rays,
for UV maybe to make violet.

Who thinks of these things?
Who knew you could eat a sea urchin?

Violet guards one border of the visible,
scans your retina, takes your inky prints

and lets you pass.
I could write a book about violet.

⊙

You think me
eternal.

It's easily
done.

Your lives are
snowflakes

landing on
campfires.

You're snowballs
in Hell,

cats' chances
therein.

Anyway, I made the cats.
I make the snow.

⊙

The damage cats do.
The hedgerow pogroms.
The examples made of shrew,
of sparrow; the redbreast
darkened to clawed mauve.

That Easter morning,
black and chill,
I stepped onto the lawn
to find the stricken Sun
pounced upon at dawn,
batted and battered,
rayless and foetal.

⊙

You shifted sarsens
and angled temples
at me.

Now you point
your furniture
at the TV.

⊙

    m   o

      r   e

         t   h

an

    t   h   e

      Sun

    o   f

i

        t

      s   pa

  r   t   s

Mercury's not ageing well,
Venus tends to kiss and tell,
Earth's beholden to its Hell,
Mars is short of personnel,
Jupiter dresses like a swell,
Saturn casts a sombre spell,
Uranus tripped and Uranus fell,
Neptune is a bathing belle,
Pluto left the carousel.

⊙

Our Fusion
Which art in Heaven
Stelliferous
From Evil

⊙

I have been studying how I may compare
the vacuum where I live unto the world:
and for me because the world is populous
and here is not a creature but myself,
I cannot do it; yet I'll hammer it out.
I know that you have found me fair to look upon,
if not direct, then by chicanes of guile,
deflections and projections onto walls
and floors and paper screens in rooms obscure,
that fetched my glory, dimmed, like tainted water
from a well. Well. Well, there's no place for me
to hide. It's no surprise that you should pry
beneath my crown to see what lies behind
such radiance, such a provocation
of brilliance. And so you found the spots,
the slow rotating maculae and reft me
of immaculacy, stripped bare for all
to see. Yet your eyes are blind to what I see:
millennia of Earthspots darkening
the globe, never ceasing, in procession,
your committees and your private sessions
planning how to bring about the perfect
genocidal rout or wreck the legacy

of antecedent cultures and their gifts
which grew in turn from blooded soil seeded
with bludgeoned brains and bones of hated kin.
To my face you lift the steaming hearts, fresh-ripp'd
from smashed and plundered ribs; pin souls inside
two wooden boats, force-feed them milk and honey
till their bodies bloat and coat themselves
in excrement, then fill their throats again,
their faces Sun-exposed and blackening
with insects nibbling to the skull and breeding
colonies of greedy wriggling young in gums
and sockets while inside the fleshy tomb
unspeakable nature feasts on increase.
But these are but grace notes in the great score:
you took your fealty, made killing fields
from fields of chlorophyll, doled out the shovels
to young men, instructed them to dig their graves
while you stand and wait, trade jokes and cigarettes,
then walk along the line collecting brains
on your lapels, your shirt-front, crotch and boots
before returning with your garrison
to the warehouse full of mothers, sisters,
daughters, girlfriends, grandmas and fiancées

to lodge the seed of conquest and catharsis
where the fucked-up logic of libido
demands it. For some that's just too intimate,
too wasteful, too direct, they set their best
minds to task on finding ways to mask
the links between the living and the dead.
A factory's the place to separate
the maker from the artefact, the killer
from the act, redact all trace of culpability,
repurpose all the spare parts,
amortise the mortified, the mortal
ties, make a burial site of amour.
Acres of tongueless jaws agape, gappy
from plier-wrenched gold, top and bottom rows
intermingled, locking teeth with those
they never chose to kiss; I've seen you drag
by one loose arm, her face flat in the mud,
a woman widowed, made childless, then worked,
then starved, then gassed, then tossed onto a pile
of evidence you thought you ought to hide;
I've watched your great leaps forward from here
and how you tend to land with both feet planted
in a maggoty pit up to your eyes;

I've seen you sign the papers cutting off
supplies of food and I've seen families
eat their dead and those who, for some reason,
want to live, roast and eat the shrunken rind
of their own feet; I've seen your oceans crossed
by villages in chains who died for work
they didn't want to do and I've seen rafts
of refugees who died for work you now
don't want them to do; and I've plotted Earthspots
come and go from western limb to eastern limb,
from north to south, from dawn to dusk, and through
the night, and there's no Earthly minimum
but one continuous maximum,
but forgive me: maybe I'm the one
blind to small improvements,
who can't move on.

⊙

I wanted to be pure and whole,
to clamp closure's gums upon
birth's nipple, keep the circle
inviolable, contain all
and yet exclude everyone
but it can't be done, the traces
cannot be expunged.

Mercury's a martyr to sunstroke,
Venus overcooks its yolks,
Earth is full of tiresome blokes,
Mars is harmless yet provokes,
Jupiter likes to take a toke,
Saturn's an elaborate hoax,
Uranus is tired of jokes,
Neptune harbours hopeless soaks,
Pluto's where our last hope croaks.

What did you do inside the Sun, mummy?
I fashioned the bells of euphoniums,
I oiled the swivel-mounts of sunflower heads,
I forged all the gongs for J. Arthur Rank,
I test-popped popcorn, de-popped it and boxed it,
I softened cold butter on window sills,
I accessorised the Kuiper Belt,
I mixed paints for Vincent van Gogh,
I drank paint with Vincent van Gogh,
I squeegeed cats' eyes from the inside,
I led the protests against sunblocks,
I pipetted cyanide into apple seeds,
I scheduled eclipses: a fiddly business,
I transhumed helium from valley to hill,
I ran outreach sessions for coronal ejections,
I campaigned for the closing of sweatshops,
I patented the highlighter pen,
I glued facets onto mirror balls,
I was a judge on *The Oort Factor*,
I invented vitamin D,
I wrote a green paper on the uses of chlorophyll.
Why didn't you stay inside the Sun, mummy?
I had to leave to find your daddy.

⊙

Slip the Haliborange of the Sun
under your
tongue
let it

d   s

                    i

          s   o

    l   v

                    e

⊙

Some people just get me.
Cecilia H. Payne, for one,
absorbed in absorption lines,
speculating upon spectra,
ionising wisdom,
righting its electrons,
taking pains to see
that H was central to
herself, and me.

⊙

Mercury's a cast iron vault,
Venus thinks it's Mars's fault,
Earth dabbles in the occult,
Mars is mangy, tends to moult,
Jupiter's a catapult,
Saturn tries to be adult,
Uranus reels from an assault,
Neptune uses too much salt,
Pluto left to join a cult.

⊙

Salve Regina, Mother of Orbits, our life, photosynthesis, and our hope. To thee do we cry, poor banished children of Terra, to thee do we send up our sighs, morning and evening, in this penumbra of tears. Radiate, then, gracious advocate, waves of mercy, and after our exile show unto us the blessed fruit of thy core, Light, O clement, O loving, O sweet Virgin Sol.

⊙

Each day I watch *The Green Ray*
and then watch for the green ray
above the bay, atop the cliff,
listening to the hiss of surf,
staring down the Sun,
thinking *this*,
this is the one.

⊙

The Sun slips off
its hi-viz vest
at the water's edge
out west.

A pre-dawn fisherman finds it,
reads the legend:
How's my shining?
Call +394500121121

⊙

i.m. Nigel Pickard

There are so-called *hyper-giants* out there
whose least flux or flare
would strip you bare
of all pretension, pride, contentment.

There are those whose most modest claim
would put your life's work to the flame,
who in a moment's inattention
seed the universe
with all the loving matter that it needs
to build life.

Too generous,
they blaze through their store
at thrice our pace,
outshine their galaxy, their birthplace,
contract our silly notions of limits, of
space.

⊙

Neutron stars
are the spin doctors
of the universe,
never neutral,
centrifugal,
fairly frugal
with the facts,
it's wise to weigh
their words:
one syllable
is denser
than every tale
that occurred
shrunk down
to this full stop.

⊙

Mercury likes to cut it fine,
Venus never will be thine,
Earth is waiting for a sign,
Mars is the dividing line,
Jupiter thinks himself divine,
Saturn's rings are by design,
Uranus is in decline,
Neptune can't recall sunshine,
Pluto's out of sight, and mind.

⊙

They used to live in awe of me:
the godhead, the fulcrum of perfection,
the prime mover, the alma mater,
the chief creator who could ripen grapes
as an afterthought, bringing culture
and savour, and civilisation.
Now I'm just the buoy, the marker
that indicates the exit from the harbour,
something to be got past,
something of a feather in one's cap,
something to be got under one's belt,
to be pocketed, regarded perhaps
as a useful pointer, a fond memento.

⊙

Mercury's a 'close talker',
Venus is a jilted stalker,
Earth is my unmarried daughter,
Mars is over-fond of slaughter,
Jupiter should trim down, he oughta,
Saturn set her snares and caught ya,
Uranus causes childish laughter,
Neptune is a poetaster,
Pluto courts its own disaster,
the Kuiper Belt's a sticking plaster,
interstellar space is vaster
than your dreams of the hereafter.

⊙

Keep supernovae in a closed tin or box.

Read the instructions carefully using a standard candle.

Light supernovae at arm's length using a taper or supernova
lighter.

Stand well back.

Never go back to a lit supernova.

Never put a supernova in your pocket.

Never throw supernovae.

Ensure that children are supervised at all times around supernovae.

Light supernovae one at a time and be very careful when handling
them.

Dispose of supernovae in a bucket of water as soon as they are
finished.

Keep all pets and animals indoors.

Alcohol and supernovae do not mix.

You must be over 18 to buy supernovae; proof of ID may be
required.

⊙

Attend to your tenderest letters and cards,
observe the billets-doux and don'ts,
box them, bind them, keep them dark,
don't prop them in full view on window sills,
for I can't help myself: I will peer and rummage
and re-read, obsessively, finally purloin
from under your nose, those words
that meant so much, that brought such hope,
that got you through this, leaving blank
screens, vanished names, traceless
traces of beloved words, the whorls
of minds and hearts and thoughts,
Sun-bleached, Sun-leeched, Sun-gone.

atapushidhavetosaythatMalevic
hwasmyfavelikemeasupremacist
atheartbutflippedblinkedboxede
mbossedbuildingeyetrapsguilloti
ninglightgrantingrespiteforlongs
ufferingsightrevealingdeeppeace
ofdarkmatterwhatmatterwhatm
atterswhomattersnomatternothin
gmattersomethingdidoncematter

☉

Sunrise gets me giddy
as a hound dog driven silly
by its master's late return.

Sunset sees me shackled
on a hilltop, in a lay-by,
with the Moon a pale ID disc.

⊙

I fear my nature. I am too full
of th'evaporated milk of human kindness.
Humankind, they tell me, is a species
of oxymoron. Oxymorondias.
How does that old song go?
Distraught in the desert, pinned at the ankle,
brooched through the eyeballs. A sure way
to let the universe in is claw your sockets clean
of meat and let photons inphest.

I am hèavy bored of this ancient light:
its grindingly slow revelations,
irrelevant phantoms, senescent
eminences of waning stardom.

I want new light, sui generis,
my own suns and planets, not these
exhausted hand-me-downs, this nuclear ash,
this landfill trash. I can do such maths
as dreams are made on.

I am the unholy Trinity, separately
assembled in distant divisions:

my ego, super-ego, insidious id
delivered by truck, by plane, by radiation-shielded armoured train.

Protest me all you like, I petition ye
to e-petition me.

This is my beauty, eat of it.
This is my beauty, drink of it.
This is my beauty, die of it.

Leave your shadow on the wall as you leave.
Do this in remembrance of me.

⊙

You're clever as Cassini
as Voyager

                          it hurts me that you're leaving

but you know the great red spot
on Jupiter?

                          it's not a storm

You of all people might have
caught on

                          it's Jupiter's Holy Land

⊙

Laudato sie, mi Signore, cun tutte le tue creature
Spetialmente messor lo frate sole
Lo qual jorna et allumini noi per loi.
Et ellu e bellu e radiante cun grande splendore:
De te, Altissimo, porta significatione.

St. Francis of Assisi, from 'Cantico delle creature' (c. 1224)

Praise be to you, my Lord, and all your creatures,
especially our lord and brother, the Sun
who brings for us the light of day through you.
And he is beautiful and radiates extravagant brilliance
and bears the image of you, Most High.

My Lord, let us praise you, with all your creatures,
particularly our brother and master, the Sun
who makes day and brings light from you.
Oh, he is beautiful and radiant and splendid
and takes his looks from you, Lord.

Praise, Sir, for you and your creatures,
but mostly for master-brother Sun
who makes our day through you
and simply radiates gorgeousness

and *really* takes after you.

Respect to you and the whole beastly crew
and a special shout-out to the Sun
who dishes out your daylight.
He is *so* fine
and has carried you a long way.

Praise
Sun
Day

P
Rays
U

⊙

The summit of your art was the sonnet,
think upon it: not many to the pun
–net, not many to the Ezra Pound. Zounds!
The rhymes would start off far apart: two poles
whose pull would overarch the ventricles
of metrical art, but soon the field lines
declined to stay defined and tended to
incline towards the taut sublime. In time
the pressure of internal rhyme would snap,
flash, backlash, clash, trash, crash, reduce to ash
and herald the new age of minimum,
in which we found the chance to start again
in calm iambics, blank of verse, and free
from all the fever of lost energy.

You like to think you're seeing the same Sun
set, although circumstance has set you both
apart. Look up, connect, triangulate,
count off the minutes and the seconds that
illustrate the parallax of your hearts.
The Sun is not the same. Each second sees
the loss of more mass than you can conceive
and even though your skin and eyes deceive
you to think that this doesn't matter, it's
spelling out the end, it's reminding you
that the energy of love you expend
is so much solar wind, which your dear friend
staves off, because it's all too much for her.
Your love's a furbelow. An aurora.

⊙

One born to be
stared at, consumed by eyes
that I evolved
from dimmest times of patchy pigment
on some slow-responding stalk
caught between
the slime and sloth
that failed to shake off
some barely light-refracting murk,
mistook this chance for progress.

One born to be
beheld by chasm-buried bugs
that felt a particle pass
from warm to cool
and twitched their tiny bulk
from present nook of peril
to a nicer nook of accidental harbour
and cluelessly passed on
half-blind stumblings
to a later slate of same.

One born to be

spied upon and scrutinised
by lucky dimples kneaded into slubs
of epithelial elasticity till they can tell
or think they tell
the angle of approaching threat,
the great and wondrous
what-comes-next?

One born to be
cabin'd, crib'd, confin'd
within the sluggish jelly
clinging to the cauldron-sides
that conjure up the fevers
and the phantoms they will later
christen 'mind'.

One born to be
focused, imprismed,
made slave of evidence,
doxy of remembrance,
of false witness, of disseminated
hatred and the pixelated
faces weeping tears of blind Hosanna.
Deliver me.

not

even

light

escapes

⊙

...of comfort no man speak,
let's talk of gravity, wormholes, nebulae;
make dust our photons and with pathless rays
shadow sorrow on the bosom of the Earth.
Let's choose executors and talk of wills —
and yet not so; for what can we bequeath
save a grinding of celestial gears, spasms
of affrighted gas, the bloating of a corpse
on the battlefield of space, rifled by crabs
of crushing conscience, all the weight of guilt
I held at bay through this long middle age.
For God's sake, let us sit upon the ground
and tell sad stories of the death of stars.
How some have run upon their iron swords,
like Romans carving nought into their breasts;
some haunted by the comets they have lured
by making eyes across the void to guide
their suitors to a fiery death; some drained
of life's blood by vampire lover; those
conflagrating through their store with no regard
for future days; some crushed by failed ambition,
turning tail and shrinking down to hide,
dragging their vain light with them, so singular

was their pride; some lost in Time, so distant
from their prime and now they fade, decline;
all murder'd, for within the hollow crown
that rounds the mortal temples of a star
keeps gravity his court and there the antic squats,
scoffing his state and sucking at his pomp,
allowing him a flare, a little storm,
to synthesise, be fear'd and kill with rays,
infusing him with self and vain conceit,
as if plasma, which walls about our core,
were brass impregnable, and humour'd thus
comes at the last and with a little pin
bores through photosphere wall, and farewell star!

INDEX OF FIRST LINES

ACKNOWLEDGEMENTS

I'd like to thank the editors of the following publications, in which some of these poems have appeared: *Magma*; *painted, spoken*; *New Scientist*'s spin-off magazine *Arc Infinity*; Antonio Claudio Carvalho's *p.o.w.* series; *The New Concrete: Visual Poetry in the 21ˢᵗ Century* (Hayward Publishing, 2015).

'The Universe Hurts' was written at the request of the South Bank Centre for The Hayward Gallery's 'Light Show' exhibition in 2013. 'I fear my nature' was written for 'Negative Capability', which was performed at Keats House and at Ledbury Poetry Festival in 2014.

I am indebted to the staff of the Mullard Space Science Laboratory; the National Solar Observatory at Sunspot, New Mexico; and the English and Astronomy departments of New Mexico State University, Las Cruces for information, conversation, and fun. I would also like to thank Arts Council England for supporting my research and travel for Sunspots.

Special thanks go to Isobel Dixon, Lucie Green, Chris McCabe and Liane Strauss. And finally, my warmest gratitude to Pinuccia Vianini for her enthusiasm, hospitality and frequent provision of a place to write.